GOOD DOGS
FROM THE LAND
OF BAD THINGS

Michael Cutter

ISBN 978-1-68197-163-6 (paperback)
ISBN 978-1-68197-164-3 (digital)

Copyright © 2016 by Michael Cutter

All rights reserved. No part of this publication may be reproduced, distributed, or transmitted in any form or by any means, including photocopying, recording, or other electronic or mechanical methods without the prior written permission of the publisher. For permission requests, solicit the publisher via the address below.

Christian Faith Publishing, Inc.
296 Chestnut Street
Meadville, PA 16335
www.christianfaithpublishing.com

Printed in the United States of America

Marvin in a snowstorm, guarding. The more I
learn about people, the more I like dogs.

This book is dedicated to the sheepdogs of the world. I was once told there are two kinds of people in the world—sheep and wolves. The sheep are the majority and believe anything the talk show called a cable news network tells them, and the wolves take advantage of the sheep's nature and prey on them. Anyone who fought for his or her country will attest to a third type of person in the world—the sheepdog, "one that guards the flock". Approximately 9 percent of Americans were in uniform during WWII. That generation, often called the greatest generation, changed the country for the better. Approximately 1 percent of Americans were in uniform for OEF (Operation Enduring Freedom) and OIF (Operation Iraqi Freedom). These men and women served their country in intolerable conditions and against an inhuman enemy. Either they stayed on the FOB (forward operating base), or they never saw one and stayed on patrol, kicking in doors and putting boot to ass for God and country. They are the sheepdogs of our generation, and if America wants to stay the country it was destined to be, we should wake up and listen to what they have to say! This book is dedicated to them and the process of becoming whole again.

The Land of Bad Things

Pretty much every book I've ever read had all the pictures in the middle like an Oreo cookie. Well, I like pop-up pictures and primary colors, so they are dispersed liberally throughout this book. I also have half-timers and ADD, so there is a short explanation by each picture.

Twenty-thousand-pound VBIED detonated next to an OGA camp in Kabul two miles north of the international airport in October of 2012. I don't think it even made the news. Twenty thousand pounds is the size of the charge in the MOAB (Mother of All Bombs) the United States dropped from C-130s while trying to kill Osama bin Laden before he got out of Afghanistan in 2001.

Blasts, bullets, and ambushes, rockets, mortars, and indirect fires—tools of the Taliban and al-Qaeda. Besides these, you get to learn fun, interesting facts about our host nation, like honor killings and dancing boys and how they produce 90 percent of the world's heroin. Afghanistan is not a nice place to be if you were an Afghan, but as an American, it is downright hostile. That is not to say that all or even most of the people who live in Afghanistan are bad. I met some great people in Afghanistan who loved their families and wanted a better life. I went to provinces where I even felt safe in town. Bamyan comes to mind. Unfortunately, it is not these people or even this province that is in charge of the country. The Afghan saying is, "Me against my brother, my brother and I against my family, my family and I against my tribe, my tribe and all against all other tribes, and all tribes against an invader." Well, guess what America is seen as over there? It's pretty easy to imagine what I would be doing if I had foreign helicopters hovering over my house every day with mini guns pointing at me while people were kicking in the door. I'd probably be pretty pissed off also. But by the same token, I would not put up with one of my neighbors making plans to fly a plane into the World Trade Towers. This is not the story about how pitiful Afghanistan is. Nor is it a story about how horrible the Taliban and al-Qaeda are. There are lots of books about both of these subjects by card-carrying smart guys who, no doubt, can explain it in better words than "Kill 'em all, let God sort them out." This is the story of a couple of dogs and their incredible journey out of the land of bad things and how, with the help of some incredible groups of people, they made an epic journey.

In this book, I try very hard not to name any of the characters who are still in Afghanistan. I name the organizations that get dogs out of Afghanistan. Tigger House in Kabul and the Puppy Rescue Mission are incredible angels on earth. They perform miracles.

I had to go through the pages several times to take out names and to take out some of my emotions. In the land of bad things dogs were not allowed in military camps. Soldiers, sailors, airmen, and marines are not allowed to have dogs in camp. The theory behind this is that the dogs may be diseased and become dangers to their owners. The other problem is that there are MWD's (military working dogs) on the bases. These animals are amazing and save the lives of our military members every day. Now no one wants to get in between two dogs when they are fighting. The MWD's cost a lot ""of time and much of your hard-earned tax dollars, and having a bunch of mastiffs on the base that can weigh up to two hundred eighty-five pounds and are used primarily as fighting dogs in Afghanistan are not conductive to having a bunch of seventy-five-pound double-alpha MWD's around.

Emotions are high on both sides of the fence about MWD's. The right wing can't get enough of them. They flat out save lives and perform tasks that cannot be done by mere humans. The left wing wants to know if the dogs want to perform as soldiers and who pays for their training and benefits. The dogs themselves live to perform. They are not food or snack driven but are performance driven. If you were to deny them their nature, you would probably be performing an act against them crueler than letting them go to war.

Now the fix to this in the States is to get your dog his vaccinations. In Afghanistan it is illegal for any military veterinarian to treat a local dog. I mean, hey, you can't have them on the base in the first place, so it is pushing it even further to have a dog on base that you are taking to the vet. If you take a dog to a military vet, they are supposed to put the dog down immediately. After all, your tax dollars are going to support the Afghan army and police department; how much more do you have to pay for? I do not know of a single military vet who did this. God bless them!

With all this going on, there are traps set out to catch the wild dogs and jackals running around the base, and then there are roaming vehicles with mounted soldiers who drive around, shooting dogs.

Now despite all this, there are soldiers, marines, airmen, and sailors who will not be dehumanized to this extent. "It is man's sympathy with all creatures that first makes him truly a man." This quote from Albert Schweitzer, the Nobel Peace Prize winner, pretty much sums it up. Despite adversity, general order number one, and a war going on, there are still people out there being people and having feelings.

These soldiers, airmen, sailors, and marines find a dog or dogs in need, and the animal reminds them of a pet at home or when they were a kid or just a feeling of being human. That compassion comes out, and they remember or connect with Schweitzer's quote, and they remember what it is that makes them truly human. Then they start the frantic search for a way to get the animal out of the land of bad things and off to the land of Big Macs and Oprah.

This is one of those stories. Throughout this book my emotions will rise and fall as I remember frustrations and successes. Throughout this book it was not *I* but *we* who made this all happen. Sit back, enjoy, and let's have a little adventure.

Oh yeah, this is not a kid's story. If they have read up to here, they probably won't have any permanent side effects. If they go on to the next chapter, I make no promises.

Bleeding Out

Sammy dreaming of better days in Kunduz.

Sammy was on the road, bleeding out. She had been cut from ear to ear and left to die by someone or ones who believed that dogs were unclean animals. For some reason, she caught the eye of someone in the convoy, and they stopped to pick her up. She was brought back to the OGA (Other Governmental Agency) Compound in Kunduz, and the medics stitched her up and gave her (and themselves) a second chance at life.

Have you ever been bone weary? I'm talking about cumulative fatigue where not just your body but also your mind and soul are too tired to care, and sleep won't come even though you feel like the walking dead. Now imagine a big fluffy dog bounding up to you with a kiss and a tail wag. If you have been around dogs, you know they don't judge. They are the epitome of trust and love. There are many emotions to be experienced in Afghanistan—hate, fear, mistrust, curiosity, brotherhood, and the greatest of all these is love. The only two that will heal you are brotherhood and love.

A dog doesn't judge you. He won't steal your girl while you are on deployment for a year or drink your last beer in the fridge that you have been looking forward to all day long. He will sit and listen to you no matter if you go off on a rant about whatever political evil is befalling the land or if you just sit there wondering how everything got so crazy.

A dog will steal your combat boots when you leave them outside your hooch to dry some of the sweat out of them so you won't get trench foot and watch your feet rot before your eyes. Boots are pretty important in Afghanistan, and grown men can become very animated when discussing whether Oakley or Merrell has more advantages in one-hundred-twenty-degree weather (Oakley). So when you walk outside in the morning and find them missing, it can tend to agitate you a little bit. When you find out the camp dog took them, you are still pissed until the next newbie comes in, and you watch it happen to him and laugh like a pack of hyenas as you watch said dog plot the crime out in his or her mind.

A dog has understanding eyes. For some reason, you know they comprehend and commiserate with you over your ex-wife burning all your stuff in the driveway as she plots her next vacation with the new love of her life, who will be off probation in a couple of months for dealing meth to teenagers, and they sell your Harley to pay for the divorce lawyer, who will try to take you for everything you have for being an insensitive killing machine with PTSD and driving her to do this after your tenth deployment to a war zone to pay the bills, because the economy is in the Dumpster and you can't get a job at home. But I digress.

A dog doesn't judge when you come back in from lighting up a tree line where you were taking fire, and it was pinning your buddies down and chewing them up into hamburgers even though you're not quite sure who everyone was in that tree line. They come up to you and still give you that kiss and sit down by your stinking body and look at you with those understanding eyes that say, "Go ahead, tell me all about it, I care what happens to you."

Now imagine, some sick SOB has decided that this same dog poses a threat to you and is not your only link to salvation and sanity. That same (fill in the blank) _____ decrees that all dogs are to be trapped and killed or shot from a truck. Now welcome to the reality of Afghanistan and Iraq. So when you get back and look for your buddy to download some heavy baggage on, and you find out some ass clown greased him because of general order number one, it tends to be a real bummer. Sorry if you were one of those jackasses who enforced that order and are looking for an apology. Come by the house, and I will do my best to express my apology to your grill. Go tell yourself how you were serving the common-good cause that doesn't fly around Joe.

Sammy became the mascot around the base. She was a happy-go-lucky guard dog, and she was unfixed. As such she became the camp dog follower. SF teams' dogs were wearing patches on their vests that said, "I banged your bitch." And Sammy likes Belgians better than Germans. It was all good, clean fun. Meanwhile, she patrolled the post with vim and vigor. She was nocturnal and was not a fan of Taliban look-alikes. She had some pretty serious baggage she was dragging around, what with getting her throat slit and stuff; she was not very trusting of the locals.

She was endearing to the base and anyone who came on the base. That dog ate better than a four-star general.

Sammy getting a treat or, possibly, being scolded for stealing somebody's boots. I can't honestly remember which one it was, but the flip-flops lead me to believe the latter. This little dog produced more smiles than ice cream.

Sammy lived outside and wanted nothing to do with inside. Everyone was just happy to have her around. She barked from sundown to sunup whenever anything moved on the base. She was a proper guard dog that brought a smile to everyone's face.

THE STUFF MEMORIES ARE MADE OF

(The kids can come back on this chapter.)

Chica in 2010. Chica at the picnic table in
Kunduz in September of 2010.

Sammy in September of 2010 in Kunduz. This was
the only time after a week that I got to pet her.

In September of 2010 we were at Kunduz, Northern Afghanistan, OGA (Other Governmental Agency) base. We were out of home base and running free. There were some missions that needed doing up north, so we were over the high pass at twelve thousand five hundred feet and up at the small base of Kunduz.

They had food, Russian remnants, a range we could shoot at, and *dogs*! This was the first time I met Sammy. I was not in the convoy that rescued her. She was a reclusive little dog, who did not want a lot of contact, but she was a dog, and that was better than anything we had.

Chica was Sammy's daughter, and her dad was a Belgian Malinois, who worked with one of the SF teams up there. All the ODAs claimed their dog was Chica's dad, and who was I to question them? It didn't matter to me as long as I had a dog to hang out with.

There was other stuff to do up there, like go out on missions, workout, and practice your shooting skills, and just be, but the best was hanging out with a dog! Man, that was something we could not get anywhere else.

Every boy needs a dog—someone he can talk to, walk with, and take care of. He gets to see the playfulness of a puppy and the growing and maturing process and then experience the heartbreak of losing a loved one and find out how important life is. It is a key relationship in his life, like that with a father, mother, best friend, and first girl. Without this piece of the pie, life is incomplete, and there are lessons that need to be learned that will be much harder to grasp. Once you have a dog, you will either become a dog person or not.

Most of the important things in life, I have learned from my dog. Be loyal in your relationships. A dog is loyal to a tee; he will not leave you—till death do you part—and he cannot be bribed. Everyone has their own opinion of someone else, and if they ask yours, it is only to see what side of the fence you stand on. Your dog only has one opinion of you—he adores you. If your dog could speak, he would never use the word *but*. If you use the word *but* in a sentence ("He is a great guy, but . . ."), that *but* just negates everything you said before then. Your dog's opinion of you is, "He is the best guy in the whole world"—no buts about it.

Attack every day! A dog wakes up and enjoys every day; if he is taking a nap, going for a walk, watching TV with you on the couch, eating the same food he eats every day, or getting a scratch behind the ear, that is the best moment of his life. If you wake up, the hard part of your day is over! There are a lot of people in the world, missing fingers, limbs, or reproductive organs. Their loved ones have died of a horribly debilitating disease. They have had broken relationships. I once knew a soldier in Colombia who had both of his legs and his penis blown off by a mine in Antioquia. He left the army with no pension, and I saw him begging on the street, strapped to a board that held in what was left of his parts. I have no problems; if I wake up breathing in the morning, it's going to be an easy day.

Get in the breeze. Some dogs have car windows; I have a motorcycle. Being in the wind should put a smile on your face every time. Some people pay big bucks for visits to a psychiatrist; other people just need the wind in their hair.

Marvin getting some free therapy!

Love fiercely! Your dog meets you with enthusiasm every time you come home. He jumps on you and kisses your face. He dotes on your every move. The sun rises and sets on your actions. Why can humans not treat the ones they love the same? Jesus left the world with one more commandment: "Love others as I have loved you." Dogs will give their lives for the ones they love; would we?

Be selfless. Other than begging for a cookie or occasionally stealing a combat boot, dogs do not have ulterior motives. They have no drama in their lives. They do not vote or believe in politics. There is no doggy president. They don't make long-term plans; they are always ready to go when you are. They do not want the newest collar or a new colored leash. They are happy just to be.

Dogs are not picky eaters. They will never send a steak back to the kitchen for being underdone.

Dogs do not worry. It is a worthless emotion that will change the outcome of nothing. They simply deal with whatever cards that are dealt them as they come.

All these left positive memories with me that I will try to apply for the rest of my life to all the people I will meet.

Chica doing what comes natural—guarding and putting a smile on someone's face. As the commercial says, "Priceless." I didn't meet anyone who didn't get along with Chica.

Normal life in Afghanistan. Dogs are therapy.

SHTF

In October of 2012 we went back up north to Kunduz. When we got there, I thought, *Man, Chica got big* when I saw the large dog on the wall.

This is Marvin pulling inside perimeter patrol on
the lower level of HESCOs. He could jump up on
a six-foot HESCO barrier from the ground.

The dog that I saw was not Chica. I came to find out, Chica was accused of biting one of the locals, and the base had to put her out of the compound. Her life span was drastically shortened after that. They never found her body. I was rocked. Over there in the land of bad things, you don't make close personal relationships, not when said relationship may not make it home that night. You tend to flip a switch and lock it all down till you come back to the big PX. When the dogs came into my life, I got to feel a little human for a while in a place I did not think I would. A thought started in my head, a spark of hope. This could not be the fate for the new dog I met or for Sammy.

Fair doesn't really play into real life. Nor do compassion or equity. You want to change the world; I hope you brought a lot of guns. Real life just happens. Because you train and train and lead a good life, that doesn't mean you are not going to step off the bird and blow your leg off on an IED on your first mission in the world. I know this for a reason.

A man was walking on the beach after a storm when he saw another man throwing starfish back into the water. There were thousands of them washed up on the beach, so there was no way even a small percentage of them were going back in. The man walked up to the man throwing starfish and said, "What are you doing? There is no way you can change the lives of all these fish, so your actions are futile." The second man looked at him as he tossed another starfish into the water. "Changed the world for that one," he replied.

Marvin coming back from his post. This was the outer guard post of the base. We later found, the escape hatch didn't go anywhere.

I wanted to change the world for one starfish (dog).

The new dog was Marvin. He came into the world on December 25, 2011. He was quite the large Christmas present. I know his birth date because one of my friends delivered him on this day. The same friend sniped his nuts (this emphasizes the point "You win some, you lose some" literally). There were a lot of big dogs hanging around, and Marvin was not exactly a good fighter. He never left the base and, as such, was not used to anything but rocks and HESCOs.

A HESCO is a large cardboard box filled with dirt and rocks. Marvin is walking between two rows of HESCOs in the picture above. They came in two sizes—big and bigger. They provided protection without having to fill a million sandbags like the old days. This gave everyone more time to play video games after being out on missions all day long.

Marvin as a puppy with a buddy in Kunduz. Ice cream and puppy dogs make everything better.

HESCOs surrounded the entire base. HESCOs and high earth mounds surrounded most of the bases. Then there were concrete bunkers all over the bases for when the rockets or mortars came. The idea is, when you hear the sirens go off, you drop immediately then go to the bunker. The bunker protects you from the rocket or mortar. Dogs, of course, don't understand this concept, so bunkers are great places to hang out when it's hot out, because it's usually twenty degrees cooler in the bunker. If you dig a hole in the bunker, then it gets even cooler. So when you are a dog, you dig a hole in the bunker to get as cool as possible, because as everyone knows, it gets HAF (hot as fuck) in Afghanistan. Now most of the time, it is dark when the mortars and rockets come. So now it's dark, and you are highly motivated to get into that bunker, so you are hauling balls to get there quickly. What happens is, you rush into the bunker and then bust your ass as you fall into the hole your trusty dog made. All your cool points go out the window as you do so, and you end up starting from scratch with all your buddies.

Now the main seed had been planted in my head to get the dogs out; all I had to do was accomplish it.

HELP

Marvin, Sammy, and my buddy in the snow in Afghanistan.
The dogs were spoiled rotten up there and had a lot of
love. When Marvin wanted attention, he would give
you a stiff pawing, or when he likes you, he will bite
very delicately with only his front teeth repeatedly.

I was naive on the ways of dog rescues in Afghanistan. I had no idea how I was going to get these dogs out. I knew that there was no way I could leave these dogs here. Kunduz was far, far away from Kabul where I was stationed. It was even farther away from Kandahar where our other base was. General order number one did not allow dogs on my base. Adding to this, when we were in Kunduz, I was told that the base was going to close down in 2013. All the agents and military guys were glad to help and knew a guy who knew a guy who got a dog out of Afghanistan. One of the issues I started to run into was that Afghanistan was a rapidly changing political landscape. What worked yesterday might not work today. One of the first things I had to work out was Coms back at the home front. I called Actual 6 at the house (my commanding officer Blanca Mirtha Trivino Garcia Cutter). "Mommy, I am going to bring two dogs home from Afghanistan." "*En serio* [really], we already have three dogs at the house now, and you want another one?" "Baby, I just gotta do it." "Fine then, you know I am with you, whatever you are doing, I am behind you." Man, they don't make them like that anymore. My wife is an angel, and that about sums that up.

So with Big Duke Six Actual taken care of, all I had to do was get the dogs to the States. How hard could it be, and what could possibly go wrong?

The first connection had moved his dog out through the airport in Kabul to Dubai and then from Dubai to the United States on his commercial flight. I got in touch with the terp (interpreter) we used, and we headed to the airport. "May I take my dog with me as my personal check-in bag?" maybe was the best I could come up with. There was nothing that made me feel confident, and it seemed my chances would increase as my ability to bribe someone went up. I was never too confident that I was going to make it out of Afghanistan by myself, never mind dragging two dogs along with me.

I had a friend who brought a cat out of Afghanistan with him. He carried it on his lap as a carry-on and then walked it into the airport in Dubai with him. He never left the airport, and he never had to declare the cat there or clear customs with it.

With Marvin weighing at one hundred ten, there was no way I could put him in the plane as my lapdog. Sammy was about forty-five pounds, so I might get away with her. I started checking around and found out she was too big to be considered a lapdog also.

I would have to check the dogs into Dubai (import them). I got ahold of an animal clinic there for some help. Everyone was extremely nice, and I got a quote back of $5,000 per dog to get the dogs back to Texas from Dubai. Living in Georgia, I thought that Atlanta would be a better option.

Meanwhile, some friends of mine were digging deeper into the guy who knew a guy and came up with some great info. This was all I needed to do:

- Rabies vaccine over 30 days prior to animal shipment unless proof exists of such received within past year. Let them administer distemper as an added bone since shots are cheap.
- Certificate of health signed by Afghan Ministry of Health (retrievable by vet).
- Computer chip prior to travel (injected by vet)
- Booklet offering bio of dog, shot record, seal of vet, CBR# for same.
- Recommend Vari Kennel which meets IATA standards, but for plastic bolt nut as all connectors must be metal (airline requirement) so obtain kennel well in advance and search out metal hardware to change out. Be sure chosen airline accepts kennel dimensions and be aware of limitations on # of animals per flight. For if latter exists, you need to book early to ensure berth for animal to include connecting flights.
- Require clip-on drinking cups for kennel (freeze water in cups night before departure) and recommend two minimum and I can talk you through an alternative that offers availability of more liquid.
- Require absorbent pad for urine and mite consider comfort pad on top of same which absorbs dog's body heat re cargo hold air-conditioning (not so important perhaps this time of year).
- Require "live pet stickers on lower 3 sides of kennel.
- Require instruction sticker, but optional as to what instruction you wish to write in (I only specified "water regularly" as I got access to dog and was able to feed minimally). Dog

- can likely survive w/o food for day or two, but WATER essential.
- Pay attention to time frames: vaccines, time to receive kennel/accessories.
- Recommend dog go "luggage" vs "cargo" with latter being more expensive, limiting airline choices and potentially increasing travel time dramatically. My suggestion if possible is (Safi) Kabul->Delhi->Frankfurt->U.S. east coast.
- Vet willing to engage Safi to have them ship as luggage, but I can school you well if dog goes as cargo which involves other complications since Delhi is now very hot and dog leaves terminal for customs review/tax (cheap, but aggravating).
- Recommend obtaining health certificate from India Vet even if dog going thru Delhi as luggage just in case. 'Cause if dog has to leave terminal in Delhi for any reason, even by accident, animal is deemed to have entered India and local health certificate would be difference between slight aggravation and wishing you never heard of the word "pet". I have to locate, but have name, e-mail and tel# for very decent English speaking vet in Delhi.
- Following offered along with afore mentioned to get you started, but have not given your names to local vet or interpreter. This is less about money and more about determination. Estimate total cost between $1000–$1500 depending upon whether you want to utilize MCTF interpreter and then amount of compensation is your decision.

It is good to have friends.

Then we found out that Safi stopped flying to Frankfurt. Man, that whole plan just went out the window. It was turning into an impossibility to get these dogs out of the country. Now keep in mind that Afghanistan is where most of the world's heroin comes from. Roughly 90 percent of the illegal drug is smuggled out of the country. This doesn't count the morphine or raw opium that leave the country. Weapons pour across the Afghan border from all sides. As a matter of fact, in a twist of irony, drugs are oftentimes traded directly for weapons used to kill Americans in Afghanistan. So the next time you see a junkie, thank him for supporting radical Muslims and terrorist organizations worldwide. It isn't logical, but it is reality that it is easier to get drugs out and guns in than to move a dog out of a country that really doesn't like dogs very much.

We had a dog get out of the country once. Her name was Bamian, and my buddy took her home with him. I got in touch with this friend and asked whom he had used to get his dog out. Puppy Rescue was the name of the angels who had helped him perform the impossible.

It is not a good feeling to learn that you can't do what you thought you could do on your own. It is a good reality check to realize you have your limitations. It is nice to be able to rely on other people. Not all people in the world are bad. But the bad ones sure do seem to get a lot of press time.

Dogs in Afghanistan

Afghans fight dogs as a pastime for the rich and a diversion for the poor. All can mingle there in the same crowd, and there is usually no tension with all the classes being together in the same area. These are huge dogs that can weigh up to two hundred eighty-five pounds. A champion fighting dog can cost $50,000 and make its owner very rich. The two main types of dogs in Afghanistan are the Kuchis and the Kangals. It is the Kangals that get huge and are fought. They do not fight to the death as the owner will lose a lot of money if a dog dies. Usually, one dog will submit and roll over, and the owners will rush to stop the fight. The fighting dogs of Afghanistan are treated very well compared to the other dogs. They are given supplements and exercises and kept in top physical condition.

Other dogs are used as herd dogs. These dogs will fight to the death to protect the goatherds or their family. They are very calm when around the family or livestock but are deadly when they feel their charges have been threatened. More than one dog have been killed in Afghanistan because they threatened an American soldier or an American military working dog. Normally, the Afghan dog is doing what has been bred into it for over two thousand years when it protects its family, but knowing that doesn't help when a two-hundred-fifty-pound dog is trying to rip your head off.

The herd dogs are treated well by Afghan standards. They are fed and will accompany the goatherd or the children as they move about. They will stay with the herd and protect them through all climates and temps, from blazing hot to freezing cold. They are an extremely hardy breed, used to hardships and able to live to a ripe old age of fifteen.

The strays roam the land and eat what they can when they can. Unless you understand a little of Afghan culture, it is hard to understand why animals are treated this way. Afghanistan is tribal while there are areas and tribes that are quite rich; there are also areas and tribes that have nothing. Having nothing equates to real freedom. These people are living free—not the United States' "The people don't know what they want, I know what they want" kind of freedom, but real freedom. They go where they want when they want—no taxes, schools, rules, or restrictions. They may show up in the middle of the firing range you have been using for the last three years. To them it is their land, not yours. They live by the sweat of their brow and the ability to come out on top in a conflict. There is no police or government where they live, and they only acknowledge tribal leadership.

Typical Afghan farming village.

The downside is, no one knows very much about them, so no one has to account for them. When someone starts killing, there is no one to call; 911 does not work in Afghanistan. When the Taliban were in power, there was a rigid ruling system put in place, and it was mostly peaceful for these tribes. When the Taliban first started, they came to be because a local warlord had raped a family's ten-year-old child. There was no police to go. The leader of the Taliban was Mullah Omar, and he hung the warlord on the cannon of his tank. Two months later they had raised enough followers to march on Kabul. They lived by the Old Testament law "an eye for an eye and a tooth for a tooth." The average life span was forty years. There were no child-labor laws or women's rights. The man was the undisputed ruler of the household. They had the highest birth mortality rate in the world. Ninety percent of the water in Afghanistan was undrinkable. When the Taliban were in power, they did not allow pictures of the naked human body. That included medical school. The professor would have to describe the human body to the students without pictures. Imagine that one: "Okay, the appendix is on the lower left side of the abdomen in front of the abdomen and above the large intestine." Go, get it.

The Afghan proverb is, "It is me against my brother, my brother and I against my family, my family against my tribe, my tribe against all other tribes, and all tribes against a foreign invader."—pretty simple and basic. They will hold a grudge like the Hatfields and McCoys on steroids! If someone wrongs your family, it is your duty to avenge that wrong years later. If your daughter does not do what you tell her to do, it is your duty to hunt her down and kill her. If a Muslim tries to convert to Christianity, it is your duty to kill them. Man, that's a whole lot of killing for duties. When I was a kid, all I had to do was keep my room neat and take out the trash. My father would not kill me if I did not perform these tasks.

In 2009 in Marjah we took Afghans to war against the Taliban, protecting poppy fields. We had seven casualties within four days. All of them were friendly fire. Because someone's great uncle had killed someone else's great uncle, they started shooting one another faster than the Taliban were. It was tribal code. It got so we had to take all their weapons away from them when they came back in camp so they wouldn't kill one another. We separated the offenders and the offended from the unit, and all went back to normal—well, Afghanistan normal, anyways.

The other slice of Afghan life that people don't comprehend in the West is *inshallah*. *Inshallah* is "God's will." Whatever God wills is going to happen; man has no say in this matter. This is applied to anything and everything in such a manner that it affects everyday life in a way that is very hard for Westerners to comprehend. Free will is not a concept that is widely spread.

Mullah Omar was the head of the Taliban. In the late nineties some oil companies wanted to put a pipeline through Afghanistan. The Taliban were the power in this country. When they went to his house to speak to him about the possibility of running a pipeline through his nation, they could not help but notice chests of money everywhere. One Westerner asked, "Mullah, why not feed the people of your country with this money? It is just sitting around here doing nothing." To this the mullah replied something like this, "The people are in God's hand, inshallah, if God wants them to eat, they will eat, if not, then they will not."

I say this so you can begin to understand how deeply *inshallah* affects each aspect of their lives. If you saw someone putting a bomb by the side of the road in your neighborhood, you would probably do something about it—call the police, go out and stop him yourself, or help him, because you are being invaded and want to destroy the people invading your land. My point is, you would probably do something. If you are in Afghanistan and see someone putting a bomb by the side of the road, you will go to your mullah because there is no centralized government and what police they have are considered crooked. When you go to him, you tell him you see some people putting a bomb in the road. These people are not from your village, and if the bomb goes off on the Americans, they will probably wreak havoc and damage on the people in the village. He tells you, "If the Americans are supposed to die, they will die, if not, then they will not die, inshallah." That is it—all things explained; you go back about your business, life is wonderful, and there is nothing to see behind the curtain. We will never comprehend the Afghan mind-set because we have not lived there. Hope is for other people, not Afghans; what do they have to hope for? Who says they want anything to change? Can there be anything better than being close to your God? If you live in a world where the highlight of your day is not having the goats get shot, you look forward to the afterlife a lot!

A friend of mine was leaning against the helicopter with me in the middle of the desert. Some kids were playing by their tent about two hundred fifty meters from us. He looked at me and said, "Man, you know what the kids like over here?" "Opium?" I asked. "No, man, pens—that's what they love!" "Pens, man, what the hell are the kids going to do in the middle of the desert with some pens? No paper, no books, what are they going to write on?" "No, dude, they love pens, I'm gonna go give those kids some pens." So there I was, no shit, leaning on my M240 machine gun, watching this crazy dude go over to give these kids some pens they would have no idea how to use. As he got about twenty meters away from them, they looked up and saw him. I could hear the screams from where I was standing. The next things that happened were pretty much simultaneous. The kids ran to the tent, their dog burst out of the tent, my buddy ran from the tent toward the helicopter, and I about pissed myself laughing so hard. When he had sprinted back with the dog nipping at his heels, he asked, "Man, why didn't you shoot that dog? It coulda killed me." "Naw, if it had wanted to, it would have. Besides, it was only doing its job, and I was bent over laughing so hard, it would have been hard to get the proper sight picture."

My friend wasn't the only one that those dogs chased. They would come after the helicopter if we got too close to their family. They were fearless. Most of the time we would see them lying in the sun and think they were bears or something; they were so big. If you didn't mess with them or their families, they wouldn't mess with you—somewhat like Karma:

That's about it for my summary of Afghanistan and the way it treats its dogs. There are a lot of card-carrying smart guys out there who can tell you the whys and wherefores of Afghanistan, so I am not trying to explain its culture. I only lived there for six years; what do I know?

Making the Impossible Possible

I contacted Puppy Rescue in December of 2012, and they were an incredible group of highly motivated ladies who performed miracles every day of their lives. They asked me some very simple questions about the dogs, told me what I would need to do to get the dogs to them, and motivated us to be able to try and continue to accomplish this goal. Those ladies were angels. If you want to have a heartbreaking experience, get into dog rescue. I don't know how they keep doing it, but God bless them for doing it.

They reinforced what I had learned so far and told me what size of crate I would need. I had a friend in Texas who was on leave, and that guy moved some mountains and came back to Afghanistan with two air-safe dog crates for Marvin and Sammy. The push was on to get them out of Kunduz because we knew the base was closing down; we just did not have an exact date. I went to our boss and asked him permission to bring the dogs onto our base. Remember now, general order number one was in place, and this man could have lost his job for acquiescing to my request (it means "saying yes," but I love that part from the *Pirates of the Caribbean*). There was all the reason in the world to say no and no reason in the world to say yes. Thank God, this gentleman gave me permission for the dogs to pass through his base. It would have been a bitch to take a taxi up to Kunduz and smuggle the dogs out through Tajikistan.

In all seriousness, I owe that guy a big debt of gratitude and am highly thankful to him. I won't mention any names here because there are still a lot of great people doing deserved things to bad people, but he knows who he is, and I hope he reads this and knows he is represented! It's your world, squirrel; I'm just trying to get a nut.

With approval granted for a short stay of execution for the pups at our base, we focused on the next step—getting the crates into the country. Afghanistan is a very interesting place with a lot of local culture and history. Nothing just happens in Afghanistan. Fact of life—everything is possible; nothing is easy! My buddy showed up back in the land of bad things, but the crates did not arrive with him. From the States to Afghanistan was a three-day adventure through Dubai and any other airport you needed to go through. The final flight was usually the same—Dubai to Kabul, and the Kabul airport was interesting.

We asked one of the terps to go talk to the airport to see if he could coax the dog crates out of them. We had to head to Kunduz again for some more operations, and the hope was, we would be able to bring the dogs back with us when we came out of there. All that had to happen were the crates getting out of the international airport, the crates getting from Kabul to Kunduz while we were there, us getting the dogs on the helicopters, and making it back to Kabul without crashing, getting shot, or breaking down or getting weathered in—good odds in Afghanistan.

I had also ordered two GPS chips to inject into the dogs and had one of my friends bring two injectable chips back with him from the States; one of the medics agreed to help me with the injection when it came in.

We headed to Kunduz with high hopes and a prayer. Past Massoud's tomb, over the high pass, and across the river to Grandmother's house we went.

One of the Hueys descending from the high pass, going to Kunduz. There were some incredible climate swings from the mountains to the lowlands.

One of the birds descending to the river. It was so cold going over the high pass; most of the time, you pulled the guns inside the bird and closed the doors.

Getting over the high pass was an event in itself. Anything over ten thousand feet was lacking in oxygen, and the engine's performance suffered. A downdraft would send your aircraft plummeting to a floor twelve thousand feet down. As the Huey we flew in was single engine and if you had an engine failure, you had to autorotate to the ground. This involved a skillful pilot lowering the collective control to reduce pitch in the rotors. This would speed up the rotor head, and when you were low enough to the ground, the pilot could pull collective back in, and the inertia from the rotor head would keep it spinning and create lift before you smashed into the ground. Sounds easy, right? Flying an old helicopter can best be described by balancing on a basketball. As there was nothing but mountains in the high pass, there was nowhere to autorotate to. We had some incredible pilots over there. We didn't say it much because we did not want to make their heads any bigger than they already were, or they would not be able to fit in the cockpit. They had to know what they were doing, or everyone would die onboard the helo. You see, it wasn't just the insurgents who were trying to kill us; from the day the helicopter rolled off the showroom floor, it was trying to kill us, and only the constant vigilance of the maintenance department and reflexes of the pilots kept it afloat. Speaking of the maintenance department, most of all the mechanics we were lucky enough to have in Afghanistan performed incredible acts every day with nothing for the thankless. They kept aircraft from 1967 flying and fighting in modern combat in Afghanistan.

Anyways, we made it into the OGA camp in one piece, and there were the bobos waiting for us. Marvin and Sammy always greeted us with a wagging tail and a smile. You couldn't help but be happy after that.

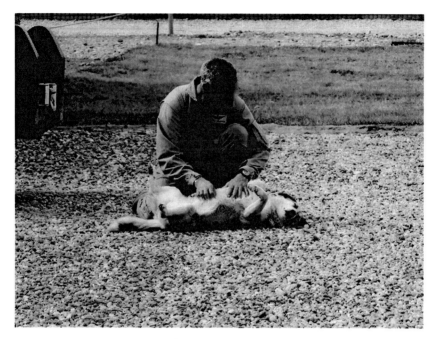

Sammy and an old friend reunited. As soon as we pulled into camp, the bobos were there to greet us. There was nothing like a belly rub to put you in a good mood.

We unpacked and moved into quarters and started briefing the missions for the stay up there. I always got to sleep on my own, whether it was in the helo, or the guys provided me with a room away from everyone else, sometimes the hallway. I snored like a grizzly bear in hibernation, something even my saint of a wife has had try her patience, and no one else could sleep when I was in the same room.

There was lots of fun stuff to do up there, and the Afghans who ran the chow hall made the best food I had ever had in Afghanistan. The gunners, pilots, SAR guys, and maintenance personnel all loved going there. Hey, it's nice to get away from the flagpole, no matter how nice your flagpole was.

We went to the old SF camp to shoot and make sure our weapons were still zeroed. SF had just recently pulled out and turned the base over to the Afghans. The Afghan commandos had sold the fuel and generator, so all the food started to rot. That brought the coyotes and wild dogs in. The base had changed drastically in the month since the United States had pulled out. "Judge not, lest ye be judged," so hey, what do I know, but the following are some of the photos of that camp when we went back there. Keep in mind, it was a fully functioning SF camp a month before.

What was left of the gym.

GOOD DOGS FROM THE LAND OF BAD THINGS

What was left of the base.

Chicken bones nailed on one of the buildings.

What was left of the bathroom.

People, I am here to tell you the place had changed. Home Television Network could not have fixed this place back with a team of landscapers and decorators. Now please keep in mind, this is just little old me talking, and I am not a card-carrying smart guy. I understand their culture, and I do not plan on going back to it. Personally, I do not see a bright shining future for Afghanistan. That is not to say there are no capable people there. I once met an Afghan major; he was one of the commanding generals in charge of Afghanistan's aid and had been through US Ranger School and British Commando School. He was extremely intelligent and knew exactly what it would take to defeat the enemy. If people like him could get to positions of power without being killed and having their families slaughtered, there might be hope for Afghanistan. There was also a female police officer in Kandahar. She was not corrupt, fought the Taliban and crooked police on the streets where they were born, and refused to go to Kabul to take a desk job despite death threats from her own family! Ladies and gentlemen, that kind of courage does not come easy, and the people she fought against every day of her command eventually killed this brave patriot.

The soldiers who were left on the camp looked like ghouls. First they had sold the fuel for the generator, and then they sold the generator. Then the reefers stopped working, so the food all rotted and spilled out on the ground. Then the wild dogs showed up and started chowing down. Then there was copper wire to be sold and anything else of value they could find on the base. They were dressed in half military attire and half man jams. Skinny as a rail, they would show up and watch us shoot and then drift away. There wasn't a whole lot of hope there, but there was a whole lot of change.

Anyways, who am I to tell the government how to spend your hard-earned tax dollars? I am sure they have a reason to spend five billion dollars a month over there.

The rest of the deployment was great, and we spent our time listening for bad guys and flying and doing raids and all that kind of great, cool stuff. The Afghans on the base were very polite to us, and the place was like summer camp with automatic weapons instead of bows and arrows.

Every morning after night missions, we would come back, and there would be Marvin and Sammy waiting for us. If he could, Marvin would have jumped on the bird and gone with us. He really liked the helicopters a lot. Somebody would have to hold him back when we were starting and taking off so he wouldn't jump in. It was the same when we came back. He loved the wind and the noise the birds made.

No, he's not howling. When the birds would start up,
Marvin would try to get on the helicopters. Someone would
have to hold him back, and he would open his mouth to
let his jowls flap in the wind from the main rotors.

Everybody took turns hanging out with the dogs, and by now, all had learned not to leave their shoes within chomping range of either of the pups.

The large crate had arrived in Kabul and came to Kunduz on one of the supply runs. Now we had the dog crates all set, and we set about getting the dogs used to them. Neither dog liked their temporary home very much. We put snacks, blankets, and even steak and chicken in those kennels. Hey, if bribery worked so well on the politicians in Afghanistan, why not on the dogs? Nothing would entice them to stay in the kennels for long. They would probably support a four-hour helicopter ride in them but not much more than that. We figured the base would be closing down in April, and it was March then—not much of a time frame to play with.

The wonderful ladies at Puppy Rescue preferred to get the dogs out as soon as possible, and Tigger House in Kabul could get the paperwork to make that happen quicker rather than later. I just had to put them on the helicopters, fly them over the high pass at twelve thousand five hundred feet, and get them to our camp in Kabul. What could possibly go wrong?

Mirtha wanted the dogs at the house with her also; no one wanted to risk the base shutting down and the dogs getting stuck up there. I figured if push came to shove, I could quit work, don a man jam, and try my luck at driving to Kunduz. My odds were eighty to twenty against making that happen. Heck, getting anyone to drive to Kunduz did not give good odds. It was very true over there that many times you just couldn't get there from here.

Marvin much preferred the great outdoors to the plastic indoors.

Now Sammy, on the other hand, was a different story. She was more approachable than before, but it was always on her terms. She was much more paranoid than Marvin. There were some bunkers, as I had mentioned before, right next to our barracks. They were made out of cement and were about nine inches from the HESCO wall for added protection. Sammy had dug herself a ranger grave (shallow fighting position), and that was where she would sleep every night. Nothing could get to her there. Now I couldn't blame her. Any human who had gone through what she had gone through would be in therapy for the rest of their life. They didn't make enough wind to take care of the problems that dog had been through. I thought if I could get her home to the house in Georgia, she would be able to grow old on the back porch, chewing on rawhide bones instead of empty water bottles and sleeping on a nice soft sofa instead of a ranger grave.

Sometimes you hope some of the negative karma you brought into the world can be cancelled out by some decent acts of kindness.

About the only one whom she would come to all the time was one of our pilots. He was a great guy and a wonderful instructor. I saw him teach the ropes to a lot of new pilots who came to Afghanistan. He had unending patience, and maybe she sensed that in him. They say dogs can sense that stuff. Anyways, his first name started with *J*, and I hope, if he reads this, that the memories put a smile on his face. It was a pleasure and an honor to work with him over there.

Sammy playing with an empty water bottle.

Marvin, on the other hand, had his own La-Z-Boy chair that he slept in most nights. The security office for the base was on the second floor of the barracks where we slept. The guys who guarded the base all loved Marvin and Sammy. They ordered cookies for them online and kept them in kibble. At night after everyone had gone to sleep, Marvin would pad upstairs and wait patiently outside the office till someone opened the door and let him in. He would get his cookie and then head off to the chair for a nap till the next time to do rounds. Now if he heard something he did not like, he wouldn't wait for rounds; he was up and out on top of the HESCOs, barking up a storm. No one was going to ambush his people at night. Marvin was and is a talker. Besides barking, he could howl and would talk to himself for quite some time. We all looked at him and said, "If only you were a little smarter, you could speak, and we could understand you." He would look back and think, *If only you were a little smarter, I would not have to!*

So as the time wore on, we were getting excited to go. Our lead pilot was going to let me take the pups out in our helos, and everyone was pretty stoked. We had the kennels up there, and we were ready to roll. Everyone was antsy because the base would be closing soon, and no one knew exactly when. The SF base closing next door was not a good sign.

The day we were going to leave, one of the big jefes from back in the States rolled into our camp in Kabul. Now I am sure he was not a bad guy, but he had not lived in Afghanistan with the same bunch of great guys and girls we had for the last six years either. Somehow, I didn't think he would see two half wild dogs running around in the camp in the same light the rest of us saw them. On top of that the last thing in the world I wanted was anyone to take a hit for something I was doing. I called our boss in Kabul and said maybe it wasn't a good thing to bring the pups back on the birds with us from Kunduz on this trip. He did not like the idea of them staying in Kunduz, but he agreed now was not a good time to show up with some stray dogs.

The guys on the base dealt well with it and promised to watch out for Marvin and Sammy. Everyone who has been in a war zone knows you are not really in control of anything. We can make inputs into the scene unfolding around us and try and make the best decision we can based on the experiences we have lived through, and that's about it. Learning is a change in behavior due to experience. Insanity is doing the same thing and expecting a different result. It does not make anything easier; it just is what it is.

We flew back to Kabul with a hollow feeling in my gut. I did not get any sleep that night, but that happened a lot in Afghanistan.

Miracles in Afghanistan—Inshallah

Now I don't know how many of you believe in miracles, but I am here to tell you that they are out there, and they definitely exist. You don't have to believe in God, but he definitely believes in you!

I have been shot twice, blown up twice, stabbed, run over, and survived my first ex-wife! God wanted me here for a reason, or heaven didn't want me up there. I believe God puts us on this earth to serve his purpose, and he gives us gentle reminders along the way to get in step with his plan, hence the "shootings, stabbings, blowing up, and getting run over" stages. I like to think back on those as God's gentle nudges in the right direction. Some people may not think it too gentle, but then again, remember his ungentle nudges, like the flood!

One of God's palettes. Even in Afghanistan we were constantly aware of his presence.

There are no atheists in a combat zone. You find what you believe in, and you hang on tight. Walk into any chow hall in Afghanistan, and see how many heads bow before eating. I was going to need some divine intervention to get these dogs home, and I hit my knees a lot during those days. Kunduz was closing in less than a month. We were not scheduled to go back there, and the snows had come. Sometimes even if you were authorized and had the means to move, you could not get there from here.

Kabul had snow, and the high passes were impassable. Aside from the enemy, the weather in Afghanistan was very severe. In one day you could go from negative five at the high pass to one hundred thirty in Jalālābād. I have seen negative eighteen degrees with doors open in a gunship for eight hours a day, and I have seen one hundred fifty degrees with 85 percent humidity over there. We once had to set down in the red desert because the base in Kandahar was getting hit with hail and seventy-five-mile-an-hour winds in April! Afghanistan is a land of extremes.

Snowed in in Kabul.

The base in Kabul was amazing. It was its own city, with water, power, security, housing, entertainment, and spirituality. Eventually, everything was there, and the people made it good. You could look at it in one of two ways. It was a jail in a foreign country that had enemies all around you. Or it was an opportunity to experience many different cultures under some pretty intense circumstances and really get to know some fantastic people who were at the top of their skill sets. Your environment is what you make of it, so why not make the best of it?

After getting back to camp, I did a lot of praying and communicating. Tigger House was ready for the dogs. Puppy Rescue was ready to transport the dogs. My wife was ready to have the dogs at the house. I just had to go and get them. Every day I was not flying I checked to see if we had a plane heading to Kunduz, because there was no way a helo was getting back up there now. Every day we were weathered in.

One day something said to me, "Today is the day, Mike." Listen to that voice when it comes! I got up and went to the terminal to see if anything was flying. There was a bird scheduled to go to Heart and Kunduz, but there was no way they thought they were going to get out. I called my friend in Kunduz to see what their weather was like. "Less than fifty meters of visibility and snowing like a bastard!" It was not exactly great conditions for a fixed wing to land in with no instrument approach.

"Doesn't matter," said the voice, "today is the day. Have a little faith." After about two hours, it cleared up enough, and Herat was looking clear. I begged a ride on the plane, and we were off.

We made it into Herat, and the weather up there was not too bad, but we went over Kunduz on the way up, and there was a horrible snowstorm we went over. "No way we can land in that, Mike. We want to get the dogs out, but we don't want to put any of the passengers at risk. We can go over the top, and when we are bingo fuel, we gotta bug out. Sorry, man," the pilots and loadmaster told me, and they were the best. They flew every day possible in some purely crap weather that would eat most pilots for lunch. Think it's easy? Try landing in an eighty-five-mile-an-hour crosswind in the dark.

These guys were good!

I called my buddy in Kunduz from Herat. "It doesn't look good, man, I can't see one building from another, and it's still snowing like crazy." Well, we were going to be overhead and were going to give it a shot. "He knows every hair on your head, why worry?"

We took off from Herat and headed into the gray. When we got to the sky over Kunduz, the pilots started a slow orbit, and my praying was in high gear. "God, I know you have a lot bigger problems on your hands right now, but I could sure use a little help here. You said that we could move mountains if we but said to the mountain, 'Move' and have faith in you, and I am saying to this storm, 'Move in the name of God above.'" People, the sky parted, and we saw the ground through the part. That was all the crew needed. "Passengers, please hold on, we have started our descent." I was smiling like a fat kid with a new Twinkie in his hand. As soon as we touched down, I called my buddy and let him know we landed. He said, "Man, I would not have believed it, three minutes ago you could not see anything. I am on my way with the dogs and the crates."

"All right, Mike, this has got to happen quick because we do not want to get stuck here with PAX [passengers] on board." "Man, G—— is on his way with the dogs and the crates." We had the big plane with pretty much a separate area up front. There were supposed to be some VIPs to pick up, but they had not shown up. When G—— and the pups showed up, the crew asked if I would like to keep the dogs in the front area of the plane. Man, we were punching out of Kunduz in first class!

Everyone who could make it from the small base to the airfield had showed up. There wasn't a dry eye there that day—must have been all the dust in the air. All the guys and gals wanted Marvin and Sammy to get out alive, but everyone was going to miss those two on the base. They had stood guard over Kunduz for more than four years. That's a pretty long tour of duty, and they had made some good friends along the way. Not having a dog to come back to was a pretty big thing. They say, "You never know what you have until it is gone," and I say that is null and void. If you served in combat, you knew what you had. And you didn't need a Walmart to get it. If enough wasn't enough, more wouldn't make you happy.

We said our good-byes and loaded up on the plane. Marvin and Sammy had kisses for everybody. They, sure as hell, didn't know what was going on, but they knew enough to know they were leaving their friends behind. There were a lot of good memories loading up on that plane, and everyone knew it. We said a prayer for the friends we were leaving behind and headed off to the next adventure. Well, Marvin always wanted to go for a flight; now he was getting his chance.

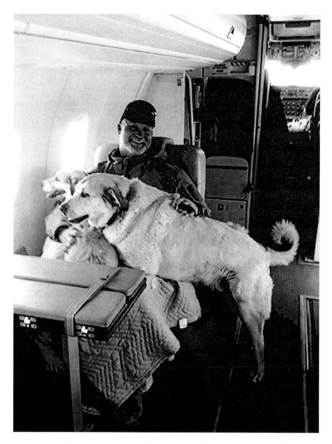

Saying good-bye to the old digs on the way out in first class. Sammy never left my lap for the entire flight. Sure hope it was everything Marvin thought it was going to be.

Touchdown Kabul

Okay, so we made it to Kabul alive. Now I had to keep it low-key for a few days till I could get the dogs out to town. We gave them a walk around the flight line, and they marked their new territory. Marvin and Sammy never missed a beat. As far as they were concerned, they were still with a friendly face and just had a new base they had to take over. "Where's the chow hall?" was their main concern.

I took them down to my barracks to get acquainted with the digs and see some old friendly faces. Now one thing I was not looking forward to was the dogs meeting the government officials we had on the base. Everyone knew what I was doing, but I did not want to rub it in anyone's face. So the first thing they did was run out of the barracks and straight to the only two government guys on the base. Lucky for them and me, these guys were stand-up prior military guys. We explained what was going on, and after making sure I had all the shots for the pups, Marvin and Sammy had two new fans.

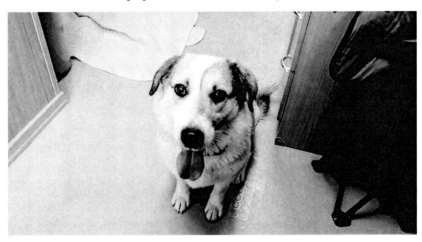

"Whaddaya mean I'm supposed to stay on the down low? I rule this place!"

Sammy and Marvin were not much into low profile. My friends came by to pay their respects, and the pups had no shortage of walkers, feeders, waiters, and admirers. Marvin and Sammy were nocturnal dogs, sleeping during the heat of day and coming awake at night. That's when the monsters came out. Both of them passed out in my room and woke up promptly at 1800 ready to go on patrol. The Afghans on base had gotten me dog food in town, and the medics came by and put the GPS tracking chips into the dogs. One of the requirements to go to the States from Afghanistan was that the pups had to be traceable. They had left the Stone Age and gone high-tech. It was a simple matter of injecting a small computer chip in between the shoulder blades of the dogs. The chip became coated with fat, and anyone who scanned it could tell whom the dog belonged to—one of the good changes to come along with technology.

One quick word about the medics we worked with—these guys were fantastic; they came from ground specialties and then were thrown onto a screaming helicopter from the sixties and tossed in a group that had grown up on helos and expected them to hit the ground, running. They could put you back together after a firefight, fix all your snivels and groans, handle major illnesses and diseases on the base, and then go out and fight off a group of Taliban operating out of a team of two—great guys to be around when the going was good or when the chips were down.

The pups were on patrol pretty much every hour on the hour all night long. "Sleep is for pussies, you can rest when you are dead!" That was their motto, not mine; by morning I was a walking zombie, so I pawned them off on another buddy and got some shut-eye.

Sammy guarding her new post.

In three days, they had to be ready to move out to Tigger House, so we all got the maximum enjoyment out of their company. Just like in Kunduz, they made themselves right at home and took over the camp. As I was out making my rounds at 0300 in the morning, one of the Gurkha guards exclaimed to me, "Mr. Mike, I didn't know we had camp guard dogs now." "That's right, Thappa, there's a new ball game in town!" Everyone they came into contact with during those three days had a new smile on their face. America uses therapy dogs in combat to bring a little home to troops overseas. I cannot state what a little normality will do for a soldier, airman, sailor, or marine. Feeling normal is a luxury that a lot of people take for granted. "People sleep well in their beds at night because rough men stand ready to protect them in dangerous places." You have three conditions: green, yellow, and red. Green is safe—in your house in the States with people who love you (and a lot of guns and ammo). Yellow is semiready to kill everyone basically every time you step into a condition you are not sure of. Red is high alert when you are in danger, and most of the people around you want to cause you physical harm. Welcome to combat. You live in the red and throttle down to yellow when you go to sleep, sometimes.

Sammy and Marvin making new friends.
Wherever they went, they worked their magic and always managed to do it looking hungry.

Everyone who saw them had a smile on their face, and I heard a hundred stories about people's dogs that they had when they were a kid. It was wonderful to have the dogs around, and if it cost me a few z's, it was well worth it.

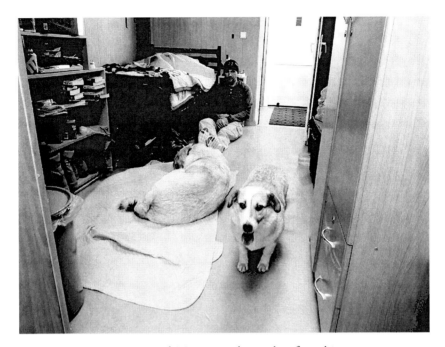

Sammy and Marvin with another friend in the barracks. It's nice to feel normal.

Everyone was very happy with the dogs except one person. The dogs had a very high prey drive, and they were used to taking control of their environment by force if need be. As such they took great delight in chasing anything that would run from them. Well, we had a group of ladies who would clean the offices and common areas on base. Now these ladies were all from the Hazara tribe, which was much farther north than Kabul. The ladies did not like dogs. The dogs very much liked that the ladies would run from them. This was great sport! So after Marvin and Sammy chased one of the ladies out of our barracks, I went out to apologize to them and see what I could do to make it up to them.

S—— was the lady who came up to me, smoking mad. I had never seen her mad before and assumed it was because Marvin and Sammy had chased one of her ladies out of the barracks. "S——, I am so sorry the dogs chased one of your maids out of the building, is there anything I can do to make it up to you?" "Mr. Mike, you are going to take those animals back to the US?" "Yes, ma'am, in less than two days they will be out of here and out of your hair. Until that time I will clean the common areas and empty the trash so your ladies will not have to come in contact with the dogs." "Mr. Mike, that's not what I am mad about." "Okay, S——, I am afraid I am confused, what are you mad at?" "You take those animals back to the US, and you won't take me!" "Wow, sorry, S——, it's very hard to get the pups out, but I don't think I could get you out of the country if I wanted to, and I know my wife would not be so willing to let you live with us." She didn't talk to me for weeks after that one. I could understand why. S—— and the ladies she worked with had death threats from the Taliban all the time for helping the gringos on the base. Combine that with the fact that a woman in Afghanistan had about as much say in the house as a hamster in the States, and you could understand why S—— was mad!

Here is another interesting tidbit from the amazing land of Afghanistan. Bamian (also spelled Bamyan and Baymian and the place my buddy's dog was named after) was to the north of us. This place had the only female governor in Afghanistan. It also had a functioning infrastructure, and you could walk out in town there and eat at one of the restaurants. We did not lose any coalition personnel there until 2012 when a convoy hit an IED close to the border. Girls went to school there without fear of losing their heads. The female governor found out some Taliban were moving into her town. She went and got the police and informed them that the town would not welcome them, and they should leave under death threat. She posted guards at all the roads leading into Bamian, and they turned back anyone who was not from there or did not have legitimate business there. Now Bamian had good reason to dislike the Taliban. There were statues of two Buddhas in Bamian when the Taliban showed up there; they decided that there was one God, and his name was Allah. Since Allah was the only permissible God, they blew up the statues of the Buddhas. Those statues were erected in 200 BC. Funny how some religions work, huh?

One of the holes where the statues of the Buddhas used to stand. It is pretty hard to conceive of something so old for a nation that has been around for less than three hundred years.

There was also a fort in Bamian that had been occupied by Genghis Khan in the siege of 1221. It seemed the khan's son had been killed by the ruler of the city Gholghola (City of Sighs, the ruins of an ancient city destroyed by Genghis Khan during the 1221 siege of Bamian).

Now the khan could not breach this city, but the princess who lived there loved the khan's son, and she came out and told the khan of a well below the city and how he could sneak in. Doing so the great one exacted his revenge on the dwellers thereof, and all that was left now was the ruins that were gradually being cleared of land mines so geologists could go and study the place. How about that for some neat stuff from the past? Afghanistan would be a paradise to go and study ancient history if people were not trying to cut your head off all the time.

What is left of Gholghola? Not much, but hey, wait and see what your house looks like in a thousand years!

The people who came to this contract were expected to be the best. As such you had a very high burnout rate. There is only so long you can operate at 100 percent before you are not operating at peak efficiency. There was an eclectic mix of prior army, marines, air force, and navy personnel all living with prior military from South and Central America, Nepal, India, Russia, Tajikistan, and Bosnia and an outstanding medic from Ireland by way of the United States of America. I remember one time going out on a mission that struck me as an interesting mix. The lead pilot was from El Salvador (the best pilot I had ever had the pleasure to fly with and the greatest boss I had ever worked for). The helo we were escorting as gunships had a Russian pilot who flew in the war against Afghanistan when the mujahideen was being armed by the United States of America. The personnel security guard who was on the Mi-17 was born in Vietnam and grew up in the United States and was a prior marine. That kind of a mixture brought interesting dynamics. You could walk through the camp on any given day and hear rock, country, rap, salsa, Hindu music, and some Russian music. Always interesting and never boring, it was what you made of it, and the people who were there made it great! Much too soon my three-day grace period was up, and it was time for everybody's new best friends to leave the camp.

Now the force protection guys were going to run the dogs out to town. These guys moved about the city in huge armored cars during the day every day. You might as well have a target painted on you. They moved everyone and everything around that city, from the ambassador to us. They were extremely motivated alpha males and females. They were very good at what they did. I wonder if Marvin and Sammy appreciated all the security they had at their disposal for their ground movement in the capital of their country.

The guys got them safely out to Tigger House, and now all that was left was the prayer that everything else would go smoothly. Hey, this was Afghanistan; what could possibly go wrong?

Tigger House worked their magic, and the dogs' blood work went off to England, where they were certified healthy. They received their paperwork, and they were off to their next great adventure.

I wouldn't sleep well until I heard from my wife that they were safe at the house.

Touchdown in the Big PX

Shopping overseas or on a military base is done at a PX or post exchange. This is where goods are shipped from the United States to combat zones and military members can go to buy stuff from home at tax-free prices. Too bad this could not happen for everyone. Oftentimes the United States is referred to as the big PX as we have a billion stores where you can buy anything. I have many times noticed upon my return to the States that we seem to be a nation that is trying to replace family and God with things. When you remove family and God from your being, it leaves a giant hole in your heart. Sometimes you try to fill that hole with things you can buy. These things never fill the hole; they are just temporary patches on a hole that continues to rip this great nation apart.

Anyways, the doggies made their jaunt overseas as well as could be expected, and again the angels from Puppy Rescue worked their magic and pulled another miracle out of the hat or from the fire. When I got the news that Sammy and Marvin were in gringo land, I stopped holding my breath and let out a giant sigh of relief. It's not easy for a control freak to give up control.

The dogs touched down in Dallas, Texas, and a finer state to enter the great United States of America there could not be. The ladies sent me pictures of Sammy and Marvin romping on grass—real grass! Please remember, these dogs grew up in Afghanistan. Marvin was born and raised on the base in Kunduz. He never saw grass in his entire life! What a thing that must have been for him to walk on something other than river rock for a change. At the bases in Afghanistan, we put down rock as a base so the buildings wouldn't sink into the mud.

Marvin on the rocks in Kunduz.

Afghan architecture is quite fascinating. Starting with a hole in the ground, the Afghans will dig down and use the clay they are digging through to build bricks on the part of their house that is aboveground. Staying partially belowground helps insulation and staves off the repressive heat. Add to that the three-foot-thick walls and a rock or brick wall all the way around their compound, and you have a house that more closely resembles a fort or a castle. Incredible people. You can drop them off in the middle of the desert, come back in thirty years, and find three generations doing quite well with a garden and fruit trees growing. If they could get to the States, they would become millionaires as masons. One of the things they did not have to worry about, though, was cutting the grass. With the threat of the warlords, Taliban, crooked government officials, and drought and catastrophic storms hanging over their heads, they were always ready to move at a moment's notice.

Anyways, Marvin grew up on rock. There were probably five trees on Kunduz, so we did not have a forest to speak of. Most of the animals he came into contact with he killed before they could hurt him or Sammy. That was the way of the base in Kunduz. Now they were on some soft green substance that smelled different from rock or dirt. What must have been going through their brain-housing groups? Most of the time when Marvin saw something he didn't comprehend, he just sat down and stared at it until he thought he could decipher it. We called it the Marvin factor. A one through five would get smelled, barked at, stared at, and wondered at. A full-blown Marvin factor of ten was a *wow*! That would require some serious deliberation, and I never knew how many Marvin factors of ten there were in this big old world of ours. We were about to find out, however, that these two had no clue about things a normal dog was experienced with.

Marvin inspecting a puppy he rode over freaking out about grass.

Car Ride

Marvin and Sammy took a ride to Starbucks for some coffee and muffins. He was in the wind and in heaven!

Marvin in the wind.

When they got to Starbucks, everybody thought Marvin was so cute, he got a free muffin. Man, this USA stuff was fantastic—car rides and free food!

Free muffins and cool chicks—man,
being a gringo isn't all that bad.

Soon after that, Sammy and Marvin were on their way to Atlanta International Airport. Now please keep in mind, I was still in Afghanistan, so my darling wife had to go navigate Atlanta traffic and find two little dogs in the middle of an airport that had two hundred sixty thousand people a day pass through it. My wife is an amazing woman; she was born and raised in Bogotá, Colombia, a city of approximately fourteen million people. We moved from Bogotá to Cartagena to Melgar to Rionegro to Vermont when it was never coming above zero degree Fahrenheit, back to Colombia to Dallas, Georgia. She learned to speak a different language, got herself a career, learned to drive a car, became a citizen, and managed a home the entire time I was deployed in Colombia and Afghanistan. Map reading was not one of her major skills, though. We owned a Honda CR-V because of its amazing GPS. It had voice recognition and could understand her accent without a skip. In the house Spanglish was the common language. We had a dog from Czechoslovakia, three from Colombia, and now Marvin and Sammy from Afghanistan.

Mirtha got some excellent directions from the ladies on where Sammy and Marvin were going to be coming in, and off she went. She found both of the dogs in their crates and got some help loading them in the car because Marvin and Sammy had no idea how to jump into or out of a car.

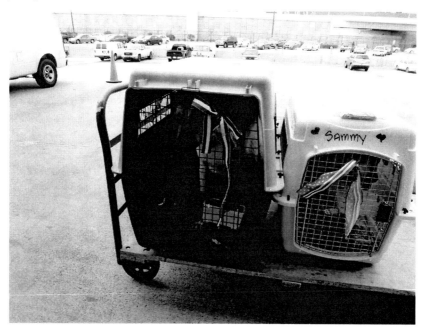

Arrival at Atlanta Hartsfield International Airport. Time to kick ass and chew bubble gum, and we are all out of bubble gum!

They were in luck because they had fallen in with a woman who had infinite patience and abounding love; she had put up with me for thirteen years. She loaded them up and headed off back to the house r introductions to the other four dogs.

Winnie was the oldest as a fifteen-year-old basset hound from Colombia; she ruled the house with an iron paw and took no guff from any dog. She kept us in stitches and was the funniest dog we ever had. She would wake you up at 0430 for first breakfast, at 0800 it was time for second breakfast, 1200 sharp was lunch, and 1700 sharp was dinnertime. All these were announced gleefully with a loud howling.

Marvin latched on to Winnie; for some reason, he adored her—
maybe because she got him fed on time three times a day.

Scrappy was the second oldest. He was my father-in-law's dog that he sent to live with us as he recognized his declining health. My father-in-law was an incredible man, and I was very lucky to have met him. He changed my life for the better, and I was honored that he trusted us to take care of his dog. He raised five daughters in Colombia, suffered seven strokes, was paralyzed on the right side of his body, and never had a bad day in his entire life. He is one of the reasons I know I don't have a single problem in my life.

Anyways, Scrappy was a spunky little white poodle that loved to be outside, hunt, and absolutely adored Mirtha; he was joined to her at the hip. Wherever she went, he went. He was a great little dog who didn't know he was a poodle. He grew up with my Chesapeake Bay retriever and learned how to be a dog from him. Scrappy was fourteen years old.

Kiarra was my mother-in-law's poodle, and after the last time she came to visit us, Kiarra stayed. When a dog entered my house, it probably would not leave until it did so from natural causes. That was just the way my wife was. Kiarra was hyper as all get-out and would run for miles every day. She was a rescue dog also and, as such, brought her own baggage to the mix.

The youngest dog was Ares. He was a four-year-old personal protection German shepherd from Czechoslovakia. When I went to Afghanistan, Mirtha left Vermont and moved back in with her parents in Colombia. After a year, she came back home so we could get the house in Vermont ready to sell and move to Georgia. Vermont is not a dangerous state to live in. In fact, it is an incredible place to raise a family. The people are fantastic, there is very little to no violence, and it is the lowest ranked state for gun violence in the United States of America. Amazingly enough, it also has no gun laws. Incredible what responsible people can do when left to their own devices, huh? The state constantly loses power, oftentimes up to three weeks at a time during winter, yet you never hear of any rioting or vandalism. Can it be that gun laws don't bring peace? We never locked the doors there or took the keys out of the car. We made wonderful friends there who helped Mirtha out while I was away. Mirtha got her citizenship while we were living in Vermont. We got to meet the governor on several different occasions, and the state was where Ben & Jerry's was founded. It was absolutely a fantastic place to live.

The issue was not the place; the issue was me. I was the problem. I had been to a lot of war-torn regions and seen the worst that people could do. My wife is the most important person in my life. I would not be able to live with myself if I ever allowed anything to happen to her. A personal protection guard dog is someone that cannot be bribed and is always loyal and always with you—in short the perfect companion. It was the logical solution for me feeling guilty about leaving my wife at home all by herself while I went overseas for up to four months at a whack.

Ares going through his paces in Vermont.
Here he is still very much a puppy.

After narrowing it down to a German shepherd as the dog to have for all my family's concerns, we searched for a reputable place to get a reliable dog from. CQB K-9 was, at that time, established and reliable, and the owner was a former marine (someone I quickly could trust and who spoke the same lingo as me). Alex assessed our needs, provided exactly the dog we wanted, and drove across the country to deliver Ares to us and train Mirtha on how to handle him safely. On top of that, he has constantly been available for any help we needed and has become a great friend. In the puppy mills out there, it is very hard to come across someone trustworthy who is just not out to make a buck at any cost. Ares continues to guard Mirtha to this day.

So Mirtha figured out where the dogs were; she came across some great people to help her load Marvin and Sammy in the car, and they were off back to Hacienda Cutter, drooling all the way.

Getting to Know You

Ares's initial impression of Marvin and Sammy was not favorable!

When she arrived home, Marvin and Sammy were very happy. Right from the get-go, they felt like this was their house. They had traveled halfway around the world on a plane for over twenty-four hours, and now they were in the great state of Georgia in April to witness spring Southern style. Down home hospitality and great cooking were what the Southeast was known for, and with all the dogs we had living together, surely, two more would not be too much.

GOOD DOGS FROM THE LAND OF BAD THINGS

Marvin and Sammy enjoying grass and springtime in Georgia.

There is a saying that all good things must come to an end, and it was not long into the first meeting that things turned a little south. When Ares came out first, everything was fairly copacetic. Ares was okay with someone if they did not pose a threat to his family. Life was very simple for him—no threat, no problem; threat was engaged with extreme prejudice. Sammy and Marvin accepted him and were able to go on about their business of establishing their presence in the backyard.

Next it was the smaller dogs; for some reason, when Sammy and Winnie met, things went south. Sammy was the matriarch of the family from Afghanistan, and Winnie was alpha dog in the house. They got it on immediately, to Mirtha's horror. Now Sammy was one tough dog; she lived through getting her throat slit in Afghanistan and living in a camp in Afghanistan. Being torn out of there and travelling halfway around the world to be shuffled off to a strange, new place with all new scents and sights and no one she knew there, she did what most would do from that background and in that situation.

The body has three reactions to fear stimulation—fight, flight, or freeze. Sammy did not fly or freeze. As soon as the fight started, it was joined by all. Mirtha did an incredible job of breaking up the combatants, and on my call home that night, I got an earful of what had happened. I asked her to keep the dogs apart as well as she could, and she did the best that she could under those situations. I had a month until I went on leave and headed back home, so the end was in sight. Marvin and Sammy adopted the backyard and downstairs; the other dogs were upstairs and out front.

Ares and the pups hanging out and enjoying life.

Now Sammy had never been an inside dog. Her entire life had been spent outside; when it snowed, she climbed under the nearest car or dug into her ranger grave and rode out the storm. Marvin had a favorite chair he would hang out in all night long. He would wait until most people had left the buildings then go upstairs and get his cookie and hang out with the security force until they went out on their rounds. If Sammy barked, he would be on alert instantly and go out and take care of business, but other than that, he was more than happy to hang out on his chair upstairs.

Sammy adopted my wife's gym as her hangout; it was downstairs and was always cool, a perfect place for Sammy to feel safe. The very first night Marvin came upstairs and fell asleep in our bedroom with the rest of the mutts, no one bothered anyone, and all was peaceful. There was much rejoicing!

I had told Mirtha that if she ever got Sammy to come inside, she had done something very special. Sammy was inside, and soon she came upstairs, wagging her tail, very happy to be home. Winnie and she went at it immediately, and all the others joined in again. Mirtha separated them and barricaded Marvin and Sammy downstairs.

Now I don't know if you have ever seen dogfights, but they are not pretty. Even I had not fully understood Marvin's heritage. Marvin was part Kangal; now if you would like to, google Kangal and you can check out how capable they really are. Marvin took out Ares, and Sammy was on everybody else. How Mirtha got them apart I don't know, but she is a very capable woman and has more of my respect every day. Marvin weighed ninety-five pounds, and Ares, at this time, was seventy-five. Mirtha weighs one hundred fifteen, soaking wet. Impressive stats.

That night she told me what happened, and I got on the Web and found a trainer. After going to the house and meeting the dogs, he advised keeping them apart until I could get back home to the house—money well spent.

Now all Mirtha had to do was keep six dogs apart that wanted to kill one another. How hard could it be?

Arrival

Time went by, as it does, and I was on a sixteen-hour flight back to Hotlanta to see my baby and my other babies. I was always happy to be leaving Afghanistan and this time even more so. Sixteen hours was a long time to spend on a plane; things like deep vein thrombosis came into play. Boredom came even more into play. You could only take so many Ambien and Benadryl, then it started to get a little crazy. I could usually sleep for eight hours per leg with the right cocktail. You didn't want so much that you were groggy when you got home or too little so that you were up for the entire flight. Ambien can have some negative effects on people and has been blamed for nudity on the plane.

Then there was the excitement of going home, leaving a war zone, and seeing a loved one you have not held in months. All that added up into one buzz that you couldn't kill. Touching down in Atlanta was always a good feeling. I love Georgia; we have the Braves, the Falcons, the highest hotel east of the Mississippi, and Peachtree Street. We have mountains, the site of the first gold-rush, a gorilla sanctuary, animal sanctuaries, the ocean, the only city Sherman did not burn on his march to the sea, the start of a two-thousand-mile walkabout in the woods (Appalachian trail), and some of the best motorcycle roads in the world. Man, if you can't find something you like to do in Georgia, you can't find something you like to do.

After touchdown you waited for the door to open to the catwalk, then you walked as quickly as possible to the customs area, and waited. It is amazing how many people go through the Hartsfield International Airport every year, and customs handles 99.9 percent of them quickly, patiently, and professionally. In a line the size of Disney World, you might wait fifteen minutes to get to see an agent.

A couple of quick questions and bam, you were back to the free and the brave.

Now with the new international terminal, after you cleared customs, you walked straight outside—no more train rides. I never checked in luggage, so I was out the door and looking for my wonderful wife. Mirtha would be there patiently waiting for me, and I would hold her like there was no tomorrow. You have five senses, and when you are away from your loved one for months at a time, you want to experience them with all five and, hopefully, not get arrested! After a while of just holding each other, we would grab a cup of joe and head out.

Taking the shuttle back to the car park, it hit—man, so much green! It hurt your eyes to see so much after looking at brown for three to four months. The water, the people, the roads, everyone walking around without carrying weapons, good coffee, the sights, the smells, the tastes—man, it was good to be home all the time every time. The bus would drop us off at the car, and I would pretend like I had not been driving in Afghanistan for the last three months and known what I was doing. I kept expecting Mirtha to clear my right lane for me and let me know when someone was passing on the right. Cars coming up from behind were reasons for concern. Always leave room to maneuver away from the car parked in front of you. What are the people carrying in their hands, what is behind the trees, what is going on in my three-hundred-meter radius (maximum effective range of the AK-47)? Head on a swivel, three hundred sixty degrees vertically and horizontally—why do I not have a pistol strapped to my leg? Oh yeah, I am back in the States where people don't hunt down their daughters and kill them for not marrying the person they were arranged to. Okay, let's keep it between the lines, listen to the newest Western country songs, and get home in one piece.

First round—Winnie, as the alpha dog, always got the first kiss. Kiarra was jumping to take her place in the pack, and Ares could not get enough of me when I came home.

When we got home, we had to do the dogs in waves. It was too much for me and them to handle everything at once. Winnie would come out first. She was an old hat at this and was just very happy to see me. Ares would jump into my arms and try to crawl into my jacket; there was always much rejoicing! Scrappy was always a little behind everybody else and a little more reserved. He was Mirtha's dog and was attached to her at the hip. He was happy to see me, but then he would go back to Mirtha's side. Kiarra was just happy to not be in the shelter anymore. After about twenty minutes with the first group, it was time to go see my other two buddies.

When I walked out back, my heart came up in my throat. Man, it was an incredible journey—for me, for them, for us. From five years prior to this, with my first hitch in Afghanistan, I wanted and prayed to get a dog out, and now here were two of my buddies sitting in my backyard, looking at me, and they recognized me. If dogs could speak, it couldn't get any better than what it already was. The eyes are the gateways to the soul and even more so for dogs. There is no lying in a dog; they are what they are and do not make excuses. Love is love, anger is anger, and enjoyment is clear. Love was shining right now in their eyes, a little bit of hurt for leaving my friends alone for a long journey that I could not share with them, and then a ton of joy at seeing me again. How did that one song go? "Man, that's the good stuff," and I drank it up.

Have you ever seen a boy with his dog?
Some things never change.

Nothing happens in the time frame we would like it to happen. Some things we would like to happen never happen. Some things we think will happen, well, never do. It's a process. This had been a long process with lots of ups and downs and a lot of times that I thought it would never occur, but now here we were. I held them and smiled. There was much rejoicing.

The first day back is always somewhat weird. I walk around in a daze and try to figure out how Mirtha arranged the house and where everything is. You live in a time warp when you go overseas. Everyone else's life goes on, and yours stops when you leave. When you come back, you step through the portal and hit restart on the watch. Trying not to be a disturbance to anyone else is a job in itself. Stuff in the house change, things break and need to be replaced, and projects you started are in the same state you left them in, so you get some comfort out of that. Change is usually bad; it means you have to do something to catch up to it. Not everything is automatic at one time. Walk into any restaurant, and see how many family members are sitting around the table, texting on their smartphones. The United States of America is one generation away from being lost. Right is right and wrong is wrong, and you don't have to be Politically Correct to be right, but being PC all the time will make you wrong.

It's funny how some people in the United States would love to remove one of your constitutional rights but are perfectly happy to hide behind the rest. Anyways, dogs are not like that; they don't change unless you think learning how to sit is changing. They don't worry about being PC either. They have a sense for bad people, and it usually doesn't end well for them.

I called the dog trainer to see if he had some time to come talk to me. He did, and he came over to the house. He walked in without waiting for me to let Ares sniff his hand. Ares bit him; my faith in his ability to train any dog went downhill rapidly from there. He let me know this problem was over his head and gave me the name of some trainers who might be able to help me out. I put the dog-training program on hold.

Sammy and Marvin were still living downstairs and out back, and the rest of the dogs were upstairs. I divided my attention between the two sets of dogs on the first day pretty well. I enjoyed spending time with all of them and tried to make it equal. I went to bed that night with my German shepherd lying on my chest and me listening to Marvin and Sammy go nocturnal and protect my backyard. I was home, I was in the green zone, I was with my family, and I slept like a rock.

The next day I got up at my usual 0300. Readjusting my sleep habits took a little time. Afghanistan was about eleven hours ahead of the United States in time, and it hit like a brick when I was coming back into the Sstates. I got up and made fresh ground Colombian coffee. I reviewed my e-mails from Afghanistan and my personal e-mail account to see if anything had blown up that I needed to address. I headed out with Ares for a wonderful three-mile run with no interruptions in the forest.

One time I was cruising down the Silver Comet Trail at 0400, and I saw the red-and-blues coming the other way. Strange, I didn't know the cops patrolled the trail here. I called Ares into a sit-stay and waited to see what he had to say. He pulled up and asked what I was doing on the trail. I told him it was day one back from Afghanistan and that I couldn't sleep, so I was out running with my dog. He noticed Ares and asked if I was armed. Now out of Afghanistan, I usually didn't jog armed, so I had no pistol on me. I told him I had no pistol but did carry Mace, weighed two hundred seventy pounds, and had a personal protection dog, so I considered my level of protection to be going for a jog on a trail in the woods in Georgia at 0400 to be adequate. He was a great guy and was only concerned for my well-being. He told me he had stopped several meth heads on the trail and to keep an eye out for them and suggested that I might want to consider jogging armed. See, now that's the change that I was talking about that I was not all that thrilled about. Earlier on this same stretch of trail, a woman had been molested and murdered, and her killer was on death row, awaiting appeals. Sometime later another woman was beaten so severely that she had to be Life Flighted to the hospital to survive the attack. Now this was in the sticks, folks, and the police did a very good job of patrolling this area. So Afghanistan wasn't the only country that was screwed up.

I got back home and had a couple of cups of coffee with Mirtha, and we had our morning time together. After that we bundled up the rest of the dogs and headed back to the trail to take them for a nice long walk. Mirtha's son was up to visit with his girlfriend, so we would take Marvin and Sammy in my truck, and the other four dogs would go with Gus and Juliana in Mirtha's car. We headed out to have our nice, peaceful walk.

Marvin and Sammy ready to head out.

You Don't Always Get What You Want

So heading out from the house was our next significant event. Everybody was leashed and collared, and all the old hats piled into the car with Gus and Juliana. Marvin and Sammy had to be lifted up and put into the truck. They did not know about jumping into trucks or other domestic stuff like that. We headed off in a convoy down the road, and before we hit the main street, Sammy bailed out of my truck headfirst while I was doing about forty miles an hour.

Now my truck was not super jacked up, but the window-to-ground height was around five feet up. Add that to forty miles an hour and throw in a dog with seven-inch-long legs, and that did not add up to a good result. I had no idea what she saw or why she jumped, but I knew she did it just like she did everything else—100 percent hard core. I stopped the truck and rolled up the back windows before Marvin could follow his mom out the window. I picked up a shattered Sammy from the ground and put her back in the truck on Mirtha's lap. We got everybody back home, and I headed to the vet with Sammy. To make a horrible long story short, she did not make it. On my second day home, I had killed my dog that I brought all the way from Northern Afghanistan to my house in Georgia. There was much gnashing of teeth.

When I got back home, Gus and Juliana were out. I broke the news to Mirtha, who did her best to console me. Then I went out back and buried my dog in the rain.

Mirtha is my peace. When I was a Marine, I always wanted to find a place that I would feel peaceful in. There was no such place. I had been to thirty-two different countries, granted not always under the best conditions and never as a tourist. There was no Shangri-La. Water's wet, the sky is blue, and politicians do not know what is best for you! Without Mirtha my time line on this planet would have been greatly reduced. With Mirtha it didn't matter where I was; I had peace. I was not the same person whom I was before her. She had a way of seeing things that I didn't.

All through this process, she had cautioned me to take my time and be careful. After a good day of feeling sorry for myself, she called me out.

"Mike, why are you so down on yourself? You did not throw Sammy out of the truck. Who knows why she did what she did? Maybe she saw a squirrel, maybe she saw a cat, who knows? She saw something and jumped. You don't control everything. Heck, we don't really control anything. You wanted to get the dogs out of Afghanistan, they are. You wanted Sammy to have a good home, she did. You wanted her to experience being a dog and having a family. She did. You got everything you asked for, you just did not get everything you wanted. Now stop whining, pick up your testicles, and go raise the rest of the dogs you brought home."

She could be an inspirational speaker. Marvin came out and smelled his mom before I buried her. He sniffed her then walked away a bit and watched me put her in the ground. Even he handled it better than I did.

Sammy, a little dog with a big heart and a ton of courage.

Life Is Supposed to Go On

Marvin, Ares, Winnie, Scrappy, and Kiarra were still kicking and barking and not about to change their schedules: 0300—get up, 0400—run with Ares, 0600—go home and drink coffee with Mirtha, 0700—head out with all the beasts again for round two. Same, same—Marvin with me and Mirtha in the truck, the rest with the kids in Mirtha's car. We hit the trail, walking and blending into the day.

Mirtha's up front with Ares, and Winnie and Scrappy are in the back with me. Everyone is up and about and out and enjoying.

What do you do when you're a guy and you have something you don't like happen in your life? You find a problem and fix it. Ares and Marvin were still not getting along at all. They would do okay walking on the trail, but in the house it was on like *Donkey Kong*. I set about finding a trainer who could handle the dog issues we had going on in the house.

Anna was willing to give it a shot. We met her by happenstance one day, and it turned out she was perfect for the task. Incredibly smart and experienced, she came over to meet the pups and said that she would be willing to give it a shot. Either of us could call it off if it did not work, but there was never a doubt that it would eventually work.

As mentioned earlier, Mirtha had endless patience. Anna had the intelligence, and I was good at lifting heavy things; it was a good combination. I set the house up like a jail; we had gates going to everything. The house could be put on total lockdown. Marvin was on one side of the fence, and Ares was on the other side. They each got their time in the yard every day, their weight pile was the walk on the trail, and time off for good behavior was given freely. I armed Mirtha with an air horn, citrus spray (dogs hated this), and regular Mace. We went over escalation of force and ROE (rules of engagement).

Anna came over twice a week to work with the pups. The starting theory was that Marvin and Ares had to be happy to see each other. They needed to associate it with something pleasant. Chicken jerky came into play. When they saw each other, chicken jerky. When they got close to each other, chicken jerky. The first command was "Watch me." This made the dog stop what he was doing and pay attention to you. This was the foundation of everything else to come. It was not training by force. It was positive, positive training. If the dogs reacted negatively, training was stopped, and attention was stopped as well.

Amazingly enough, it worked. *Zapataria a su's zapatos*. Shoemakers make shoes. It makes sense when you understand it. We listened to Anna and put everything she said into action. The dogs started to respond to it.

Marvin was highly motivated by food. Ares was a highly motivated dog, period. If Marvin was going to get chicken to see Ares, then he wanted to see Ares all day long. We would move them closer together gradually. Marvin's territory was the backyard and downstairs. Ares's territory was everywhere. Blending territories was not easy, but the front yard was neutral territory, so that was where most of the training happened.

Marvin continued with his *wow* factor. Houses barked at him; giant furry animals were next to the walking path. Trees were everywhere with tiny furry creatures that he could get close to but never catch. He started to get the hang of being in the truck. Wind in his hair was one of his favorite things. He learned to jump into and out of the truck all by himself. He discovered bones, and he loved digging. He would look out into the yard and be happy or, at least, what I took for dog happy.

Marvin on the back porch, looking out into the Georgia wilds.

Before too long, I had to head back to Afghanistan. Mirtha was staying back with the dogs. She had no thoughts of failure, only success. She made a promise to herself when Sammy died that Marvin would always have a good home. Mirtha didn't break promises. She would work with Marvin and Ares until they could be together in the same room. Anna's projection was that the pups would be able to be together supervised, but we were unsure if they would ever be able to be together unsupervised.

Marvin at one of the doors, waiting for work release to come into the house.

Ares at the cell door upstairs, waiting for his time in the yard.

Going back to Afghanistan sucked—leaving home, leaving the family, leaving the pups, leaving the color green, and going back to a jail where the safe part was on the inside of the jail, and everyone on the outside was trying to kill you. The best part of going back to Afghanistan was making it alive to your jail to ride out another sentence.

The last day at the house was spent trying to finish all the honey do's that were not done, checking to make sure you had all the gear packed you needed, and spending every second that you could with the ones you loved.

Leaving the dogs sucked; Winnie was an old hat at me going away, and she took it like a champ. Ares was not so well, and Marvin was not happy at all that his friend from Afghanistan was leaving him in a strange place with not very friendly dogs.

I gave them all a big chunk of chicken jerky and a big hug to last me three months and headed out the door. Mirtha drove me to the airport and dropped me off at the Delta terminal. She did her best to not cry, and I held her like nothing could ever part us, then we walked away from each other. For the fourteen years we had been together, that woman had been putting up with her husband leaving to go to some far-off place and do bad things to bad people. I thought she had the harder job.

Going Back to the Land of Bad Things

From that point on, you just upshifted till you were back in the land of bad things. "Lock away" emotions—happy, hateful, and hungry—were pretty much the only three emotions you were going to stay in touch with over there. Say good-bye to condition green (comfortable and peaceful with a sense of safety and well-being about you); you would be in yellow (alert) or red (high alert for the next rest of your life). My father told me a lot of things that stuck, but one that started to replay over and over was, "Forever isn't as long as it used to be."

I went back and buried myself in my work. I didn't like change very much; neither did the dinosaurs. One thing I did like a lot for a change was the Internet with the ability to talk to my family from overseas. MagicJack was wonderful; FaceTime was manna from heaven. During my days as one of Uncle Sam's Misguided Children, we got one Mars call during a six-month deployment; now I could speak to my wife with a video conference twice a day—awesome!

Well, other things were changing that I was not so fond of. The United States was pulling out, and there was no way that I could see Afghanistan staying up on its own. The Middle East was a very rapidly changing environment. At this point in time, July 2014, the situation in the Middle East was this:

We support the Iraqi government in the fight against ISIS.

We don't like ISIS, but ISIS is supported by Saudi Arabia whom we do like.

We don't like al-Assad in Syria. We support the fight against him, but ISIS is also fighting against him.

We don't like Iran, but Iran supports the Iraqi government in its fight against ISIS.

So some of our friends support our enemies, some enemies are now our friends, and some of our enemies are fighting against our other enemies, whom we want to lose, but we don't want our enemies who are fighting our enemies to win.

If the people we want to defeat are defeated, people we like even less could replace them.

And all this was started by us invading a country to drive out terrorists who were not actually there until we went in to drive them out.

It's quite simple, really.
Do you understand now?

Confused? Don't be like the federal government that spends roughly .30 percent–.50 percent of every dollar you make and hires card-carrying smart guys who can't figure it out either. Just sit back and relax as the world comes apart around us. There is very little you can do about it, and someone who is not on the battlefield is usually restricting the people who can do something about it and more worried about the next election results than actually winning a war.

ROE (rules of engagement) and SOFA (status of forces agreement)—both of those are near and dear to a contractor who carries weapons overseas. Going to jail after being tried by a jury of your peers is one thing. Getting your head chopped off after being tried by a jury of tribesmen who despise your country and whom you have been warring against for the last six years is quite another. While the military sits back and watches Congress erode their initial benefits package, the wheels of war turn and spit out American bodies and brains that are never quite going to be right again. Another friend of mine told me something that started to make more and more sense to me: "I don't need this shit in my life." I often hear the words "exit strategy." Massive amounts of time are spent on discovering an acceptable exit strategy. How about an entrance strategy for war? Number one, have a goal that can be achieved with military might. Killing Osama bin Laden, killing Saddam Hussein, pushing the Iraqi forces out of Kuwait, and pushing the Taliban out of Afghanistan—those are attainable by military might; nation building is not. The Warsaw Pact worked; being PC with a nation that appreciates Sharia law will not. Number two, once we have outlined the militarily attainable goal, every member of Congress needs to look into the president's eyes and understand that the decision is being made to send American men and women into harm's way, and many of those young men and women will not be coming home. Mothers, fathers, wives, and children will not see their loved ones again because of that decision being made to go to war. After the decision has been made to launch the most powerful military in the world, no one will walk out of that room and say, "I believed it was a horrible idea to go to war, and I advised against it." All in, boys and girls then take responsibility for your actions and back up the commander in chief. After that, cry havoc and let loose the dogs of war. We do not need the press there to document every action that occurs, from the first boot on the ground to the political after-action report of the troop withdrawal. Atrocities were committed that caused the war, and you can bet your bottom dollar, atrocities are going to be committed to end it. Hiroshima and Nagasaki were not full of only enemy combatants. You know, Abraham Lincoln once wrote a letter to General Sherman when one of Lincoln's secretaries called Sherman's tactics into criticism. Lincoln said something to the effect of "It has been my experience that politicians handle political matters, and generals handle military matters, and, sir, you have handled matters quite well." It's a shame that had to change. You don't win wars by making the other side think you are a nice or reasonable enemy. War is not nice; it is not diplomatic. It is the very last resource to be called upon when diplomacy has failed, and, gentlemen, when diplomacy has failed, please have the common courtesy to step back and let the professionals take care of it. You will hold us accountable for our actions afterward. Lord knows, Monday morning, quarterbacking has become a news and national pastime.

Anyways, I made the decision that it was time to go home. I was tired of watching good people getting their hands tied by assholes who were not even on the same continent. I guess, in hindsight, that was not a big change in recent history. It was time for DEROS to the States and back to my little slice of heaven. The people would be missed; the place would not. I dearly miss Colombia—the culture, the people, and the place. I feel like it is my second home and go back to visit friends and family frequently. I did six years in Colombia and finally left the conflict there in 2004. I can tell you many funny stories from down there when you have some time and we have a beverage of our choice in front of us. I can tell you about a lot of great people whom I met in Afghanistan, but I don't have very many funny stories from over there, and I don't ever see myself going back to visit.

For a long time when I went back, we tried rescuing other dogs for soldiers over there. It got harder and harder to accomplish. Red tape and battlefield difficulties made quick pickups and long hauls harder to accomplish. The ladies from Puppy Rescue continued to be angels, and I continued to get burned out. If you ever decide you want to try and throw an incredible amount of energy at something, try convincing the government to rescue dogs in a war zone.

Mirtha was at home, taking care of business, and Anna was over twice a week working with Ares and Marvin. They had a horrible setback and got in a fight that put Mirtha in the hospital for stitches. Now dogfights have ended up killing people, and the best thing is to not get between two dogs that are fighting. Mirtha was quite the mom and would not let either of her puppies get hurt. I needed to get home. I made the decision and turned in my notice. The men and women whom I got to work with in Afghanistan were some of the best I had ever seen. They are doing wonderful things and helping in an area that needs a lot of help. They are missed and fondly remembered. We would not have been able to do what we did over there without all the people who made it possible.

My last time packing up to go home was with mixed feelings. I was able to stay for Thanksgiving and managed to arrange to get some turkeys flown down to Kandahar for some of the people from the same team, and we had a great time. I got to spend some more time with great friends whom I had shared a lot with and hoped to see again under different circumstances. At the same time, I knew I was coming home for good to my wife and family, and that was a good feeling. The guys gave me some incredible parting gifts, and it was time to head out and catch the freedom ride home. My buddy gave me a ride to the airport, and away we flew—across the pond and back to the big PX.

Good night, Kabul, and thanks for all the fish!

Momma, I'm Coming Home

When I got back to Atlanta, I picked up my bags and gear and headed out to the passenger area and got a hug from my incredible wife; again we held each other like there was no tomorrow and were alone in our own universe, where the sun usually shone, and when it didn't, we used those times to appreciate the times it did. From there, we went out to the car, and I pretended like I could drive in normal traffic again. We went back to the house to see the boys.

My eyes hurt to adjust to the color green again, and the moisture in the air was incredible. All the stores and signs were distracting as were the lanes and directions. My eyes darted around three hundred sixty degrees to ensure my buffer zone. My hip felt strange because it did not have the weight of a pistol on it. My breathing was easier because I was not wearing an armored plate carrier. Music that came out of the radio was in English! Nobody was being called to prayer five times a day in a language I couldn't understand.

Dunkin' Donuts—holy crap—what a great store: sugar and coffee at the same place. Where were all the mounds of trash and people begging in the street? Oh yeah, I was out of the land of bad things. Women were not covered in a blue bag, and people ran around relatively unafraid.

We made it home without instance, and Ares, Winnie, Scrappy, and Kiarra all came out to give me much rejoicing. Then I went out back to visit Marvin. I could tell you a lot of things, but the feeling I got when I got to just chill on my back porch with Marvin, the miracle dog that Puppy Rescue Mission got out of the land of bad things, was a feeling I couldn't describe. Heaven would be the closest thing I could imagine. I was home, Marvin was home, and God willing, neither one of us would ever have to go back there again.

A lot to come home to!

To the free people of Afghanistan, may you keep what is so hard to come by. Lord knows you have fought long and hard to attain it. To the soldiers, marines, air force and navy personnel who fought there, thank you for your service. To the thousands of contractors who worked over there, thank you for what you did. To the members of that club who go out over the wire every day, may God and the courage of your fellow warriors bring you back home safely. It is a prize that not all can savor. As for me and mine, we will serve the Lord in peace with his blessing. Marvin has many more bones to wrestle with, squirrels to bark at, and wonders to *wow* at. May we all have many more of the same!

Afterward

Anna and Mirtha continued to work their magic on Marvin and Ares, and while they are not best friends, they do tolerate each other now and, beyond hope, can be left together unsupervised. When they think no one is watching, they can even be seen playing together! There are a lot of things that can take my mind back to Afghanistan and the things that I got to do and see there. There is one that constantly puts my mind at ease. Marvin is an incredible dog—strong, resilient, faithful, playful, guarding, watchful, patient, loving; he is a sheepdog among the wolves. I send a special thank-you out to Puppy Rescue, to Anna for all the impossible things she had faith in doing, to my wife for her patience and understanding, and to all the people who helped to make this dream a reality. Not a day goes by when I don't know how blessed I am. By buying this book, you contribute to the Puppy Rescue Mission so they can continue to perform miracles, because those people have the hard fight of coming back from the edge to a society that will never understand what they went through, so I thank you, the reader. When anyone who fought over there can look at their four-legged buddy they managed to save from certain death, it helps us to heal.

As for me and Marvin, you can find us on the Silver Comet Trail, being amazed by the color green and every other living thing we come in contact with, or sitting on the back porch, being thankful just to be alive. We continue to learn and grow in body and mind and find more and more of the peace you hear of every day. May God continue to bless you and yours, and may he bring all our people back from the land of bad things.

Marvin and Ares living the good life together
in the great state of Georgia.

Sign from the gym in Kunduz where Marvin got banned.

GOOD DOGS FROM THE LAND OF BAD THINGS

Marvin never met a bone he didn't like.

To the little dog with the big heart who started it all, thank you for guarding us, and may you rest in peace. Inshallah.

About the Author

I was born and raised in New England by some great parents, who gave me a cool childhood and imparted to me my love of dogs. I cut my teeth, so to speak, in Uncle Sam's Misguided Children. After eleven years in the marines, I packed up and shipped out to Colombia, working as a contractor in the antinarcotics biz. While there, I met the woman who changed my life and brought me to this journey with God. After getting hurt down there, I managed to be blessed with a great job in Vermont, where my wife became a citizen of this great country and God worked in our lives to bring us many blessings and a lot of learning through great people. After four years of a great job, making new weapons for our military, I got to go to Afghanistan, where I worked as a contractor in antinarcotics again. I have five incredible children with different and interesting personalities who are all healthy. I have an incredible wife, who continues to amaze me every day. I have no sand in my food, no one is shooting at me, I am not sleeping in a tent, and I will probably make it to bed alive tonight. I am highly blessed and favored, thankful, and rejoice in every day the Lord has made.

CPSIA information can be obtained at www.ICGtesting.com
Printed in the USA
BVOW02s1813080516

447262BV00001B/29/P